PUFFIN BOOKS

COMING ROUND THE MOUNTAIN

Born in Kasauli in 1934, Ruskin Bond grew up in Jamnagar, Dehradun, New Delhi and Simla. His first novel, *The Room on the Roof*, written when he was seventeen, received the John Llewellyn Rhys Memorial Prize in 1957. Since then he has written over 500 short stories, essays and novellas and more than forty books for children.

He received the Sahitya Akademi Award for English writing in India in 1992, the Padma Shri in 1999 and the Padma Bhushan in 2014. He lives in Landour, Mussoorie, with his extended family.

Also in Puffin by Ruskin Bond

RUSKIN BOND

Coming Round the Mountain

In the *year* of Independence

Illustrations by Mihir Joglekar

PUFFIN BOOKS
An imprint of Penguin Random House

PUFFIN BOOKS

USA | Canada | UK | Ireland | Australia
New Zealand | India | South Africa | China | Singapore

Puffin Books is part of the Penguin Random House group of companies
whose addresses can be found at global.penguinrandomhouse.com

Published by Penguin Random House India Pvt. Ltd.
4th Floor, Capital Tower 1, MG Road,
Gurugram 122 002, Haryana, India

First published in Puffin Books by Penguin Random House India 2019

Text copyright © Ruskin Bond 2019
Illustrations copyright © Mihir Joglekar 2019

ISBN 9780143333562

Typeset in Baskerville
Book design and layout by Parag Chitale
Printed at Replika Press Pvt. Ltd, India

www.penguin.co.in

CONTENTS

PREFACE

In the first of these short memoirs, *Looking for the Rainbow*, I had described the two years I had spent with my father when I was just nine years old. He was forty, serving in the RAF during World War II. The scene was New Delhi and the years 1941 and '42, with Indian independence just round the corner. It was a happy time for me, ending abruptly with the loss of my father.

In the next book, *Till the Clouds Roll By*, I described the sudden change in my circumstances, and the effort I had to make to adjust to a new and very different life with my mother and stepfather.

And now in *Coming Round the Mountain*, I have dwelt on my schooldays, in particular one memorable year, 1947, during which a lot of things happened to me and around me. The making of friends; the loss of friends; the country's freedom and its division; changes everywhere . . . But there was one constant—

my love of books, and an inclination for putting things down on paper—and it was this that gave me the confidence and self-belief to take on the uncertainties of living in a changing world.

'Be true to yourself,' my father always told me, 'and if you are true to yourself, you will be true to others.'

Ruskin Bond
Landour, Mussoorie
April 2019

1
THE FEARSOME FOUR

Clang, clang, clang! Bong!

Even before the sun was up, we had to be up.
Morning PT at 6.30 a.m.

'It just isn't natural,' complained Tata Junior.

'It's like being in the army,' grumbled
Harminder Singh.

'And when were you in the army?'
responded Krishnan, flinging a pillow at his
friend.

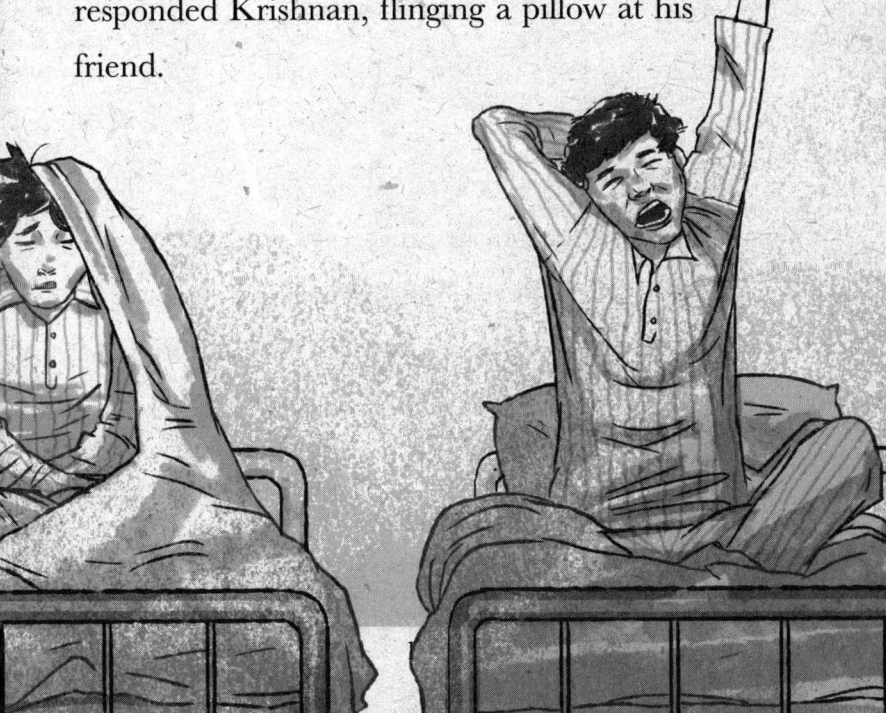

The junior dormitory consisted of third- and fourth-form boys, that is, the British public school equivalent of today's sixth and seventh standards. At Bishop Cotton, in Simla, everything was like the British public school, including canings (but only up to six strokes of the cane), compulsory games, masters in academic gowns, short haircuts and grace before meals.

For what we are about to receive,

May the Lord make us truly . . .

But before we could be truly grateful, hands would be snatching at thinly buttered slices of bread, sauce bottles and jam pots.

We were not badly fed—indeed, our breakfast was quite substantial. But before breakfast came that early morning bell—the 'rouser', we called it—followed by our PT session on the first flat.

'Rise and shine, boys! Rise and shine!' called our PT master as hundreds of sleepy boys trooped down to the flat, the first of three descending

playing fields. 'Dunda' Hawkes, our PT master, was a retired English sergeant and a former army boxing champion. At sixty, he still possessed a powerful frame, a strong, bullish neck, a barrel of a chest and impressive biceps. Sometimes he would demonstrate his muscular prowess by flexing his arms and making his biceps wobble about while he sang, 'Pack up your troubles in your old kitbag, and smile, smile, smile!'

Unlike the other masters, he never caned us boys, but he was never disobeyed. We were all in awe of his great strength and dignified demeanour.

*

It was 1947, and life was about to change quite dramatically for most of us.

I was turning thirteen in May that year. My best friends were Azhar Khan, who was my age; Brian Adams, who was a year younger; and Cyrus Satralkar, who was the youngest. We called ourselves the 'Fearsome Four', although there was nothing very fierce about us.

Since the death of my father two years previously, I'd been going through a different period, adjusting to my stepfather's home in Dehra and learning to cope with the world at large.[1] Although a shy boy, I needed friends, and I was quick to respond to those who offered me friendship.

Azhar was a quiet, soft-spoken boy. He came from the North-West Frontier Province, but there was nothing unruly or rough about him, as many might have imagined. Satralkar was the

---

[1] This period is described in my two memoirs *Looking for the Rainbow* and *Till the Clouds Roll By.*

THE FEARSOME FOUR

smallest boy in his class. I think he was Iranian. Brian's home was in Bangalore. We were not in the least interested in each other's religions or regional backgrounds. Adults seemed to think it important; but at thirteen, friendship and loyalty seemed to matter more.

The catalyst for our bonding was that early -morning rouser for PT. For some reason— or different reasons—the four of us overslept one morning and failed to turn up on the first flat for our exercises. Our absence was duly reported by a senior prefect, and we were summoned to the headmaster's study for the usual punishment. At least three strokes of the cane were to be expected.

Poor Satralkar had never been caned before. Adams had received several floggings. He was something of a hero in this respect. The more often you were punished, the higher your prestige in the corridors of our ancient school. Azhar and

I were not often in trouble, but in the course of our long academic careers (five years in junior school and one in senior!) we had felt the flat of the hairbrush and the sting of the Malacca cane a few times.

'Now, take my advice,' said Brian, from his vast background of experience. 'Slip a couple of books down the seat of your pants. Old Fishy won't notice. They'll absorb some of the sting!' We took his advice, but Satralkar wanted further insurance and rushed up to the dormitory to put on an extra pair of woollen underpants. At least that was allowed.

We trooped off to the headmaster's study. Mr Fisher stared at us through his thick-lensed spectacles.

Even when he had his back to us, he could see us in the reflection from his lenses. Old Fishy never missed anything.

'Bend over, Adams.'

Brian Adams bent over—*whack!* The cane descended, giving off a rather hollow sound.

'Something tucked away in your trousers' seat? Out with it, Adams.'

Pulling a face, Brian removed two exercise books from the seat of his trousers. *Whack! Whack!*

'Ow, sir!' The third stroke was applied with a little more energy than the first two.

'Next!'

Azhar prepared for the punishment. Fisher tapped him on the seat of his pants. 'Out with it, boy!'

Reluctantly, Azhar fished out a textbook—Shakespeare's *As You Like It*, with notes by Prof. Agarwal.

'I see you're taking an interest in literature,' said Fisher. 'Well, see if you like this too,' and Azhar manfully received three strokes of the cane.

'Your turn, Bond. But first let's have a look at what you're reading these days.'

A blushing Bond delved into his trousers' seat and came up with a copy of *The Strange Case of Dr Jekyll and Mr Hyde*.

'And a hiding you shall get,' said Fishy with a grin. He was enjoying himself. And that cane really stung!

As Cyrus did not have any books concealed on his person, he got off with just one stroke of the cane. He was very brave about it.

We all promised never to be late for PT again and sped off to the dormitory to display our wounds—the appearance of red and purple welts—to an admiring crowd of our class fellows and dormitory mates. Brian was heading for the school record as far as floggings went, his only rival being Tata, who was a glutton for punishment.

2

HOCKEY WITH AZHAR

The school term started with the hockey season. It was followed by cricket, then football during the monsoon months, then boxing, swimming and athletics. And in between we had our classwork and homework and PT and chapel services and debates and anything the authorities could think of to prevent us from thinking. Their theory was that if a boy was left alone for five minutes, he'd get up to mischief and probably grow up to be a communist or a circus artiste.

Once a month, on a Saturday, we were allowed into town, and that was our greatest luxury, something we all looked forward to. And there was no greater punishment than being 'gated', or kept in school, while everyone else wandered along Simla's Mall Road, enjoying ice creams or visiting the cinema.

Hockey was all right. Games being compulsory, everyone was given a new hockey stick, and in the dormitory we would use them for fencing bouts, like Errol Flynn and Basil Rathbone in *Captain Blood*. Those swashbuckling adventure films were all the rage.

Hockey sticks were also useful when it came to knocking down the apples in the headmaster's garden, but this was fraught with danger. To be caught meant not only a caning but also detention in school on an outing day.

At hockey, I did not shine as a forward (too much running about!) or as a full back (too much running after the opposing forward), but I made an impression as a goalkeeper, happy to rush out at advancing foes, knocking them over if necessary and kicking the ball away with my pads. No face protection in those days, but the ball was seldom hit into the air.

So it was as a goalkeeper that I made it into the Colts, the junior hockey team—a great honour, as it meant I would represent the school in its annual hockey match against our rival, Sanawar, the old army school near Kasauli, where I was born.

Azhar, too, had made the hockey team, as a solid and reliable half back, good at taking penalty corners.

It was Sanawar's turn to host our hockey teams, and we were bundled into the back of a truck and driven down the winding road to the school, a two- or three-hour journey, in the course of which most of us got sick.

But our stay in the school was pleasant enough. No morning PT. No classes. No homework. No sticky lumps of rice. Chicken for a change. For two blissful days, anyway. Azhar and I roamed the hillside, dipping into a paper bag full of jalebis, obtained from the local tuck shop.

'Will you be coming back next year?' he asked.

'Don't know,' I said.

'Independence is coming. All the British boys are going away.'

'My father and I would have gone too, if he hadn't died. Now my mother's married to an Indian. I suppose I'll stay. There's nowhere else to go—unless it's another school. What about you? I suppose you'll be back.'

'Don't know. Our home is in Peshawar. And my father says the country may be cut in two!'

'That's terrible. How can you cut up a country? The war is over.' I was referring to World War II.

'There are different kinds of war, I suppose. Different races, different religions, all wanting their own place.'

'People are different, I suppose—unless they love each other. Friends must remain friends.'

'Friends forever,' said Azhar, putting his arm round my shoulder. 'So what shall we do now?'

'Get more jalebis,' I said.

*

The match was in the evening, and we still had time to ourselves. We wandered into the school chapel. There, on the honours board, was my father's name—Flt Lt A.A. Bond—along with the names of others from Sanawar who had lost their lives during World War II.

I felt very proud to see his name up there. I remembered the long hot summer and the two winters we had spent together in New Delhi—waiting for him in an Air Force hutment, sorting through his stamp collection, going to the pictures, taking tonga rides, making plans . . . And then suddenly, with his death, everything had changed, and life had gone on but in a totally different direction.

'Never make plans,' I said to myself.

'What did you say?'

'I said, never make plans. They are bound to go awry.'

'All the same, we have to plan something. Like tomorrow's match. How we're going to win it!'

*

It was a good hockey match, evenly contested. In the first ten minutes we were awarded a penalty corner, and Azhar shot low and wide, giving the goalkeeper no chance. After that the Sanawar team made several attacks on our goal, and I was kept very busy making several saves or charging out to kick the ball away. And all the time the cheerleaders from the Sanawar girls' school were chanting away and cheering on their players, while we had only a handful of supporters in the stands. Ours was an all-boys school; no screaming girls to inspire us! Late in the game they scored an equalizer when I misjudged a scoop from their centre forward.

INTER-SCHOOL
HOCKEY MATCH

SANAWAR	BISHOP
01	01

The game ended in a draw, and I wasn't too disappointed with the result. I'd made several good saves. And, after all, we were playing against my father's old school.

'You must feel proud,' said Azhar, who was standing beside me as we prepared to leave.

'Yes, he was the best of fathers. But I'd rather he were alive and waiting for me at home.'

Do wars solve anything, I wondered, or do they just lead to more wars?

It was late evening when the truck took us back to Simla. We kept singing all the way back—noisy, naughty songs that we had picked up from the troops during the war years.

She'll be coming round the mountain when
    she comes,
She'll be wearing silk pyjamas when she comes!

And:

Rolling home, rolling home,
By the light of the silvery moon . . .

And the moon came out and saw us all the way
back to school.

3
ENTER A GIRL

Clang, clang, clang! That rouser (or gong) never stopped ringing. It got us out of bed, it summoned us for meals, it rang between class periods, it sent us unwillingly to bed.

One morning it failed to ring, or rather, there was no bell to ring. Someone had removed it, and it wasn't found till late in the afternoon.

What a glorious day! As there was no bell to rouse us, everyone got up late, and there was no morning PT. Some of us missed breakfast too. The teachers got confused and mixed up their classes. Dunda Hawkes organized a treasure hunt and sent some fifty boys down the hillside in search of the bell. How could the school manage without it? Confusion reigned. The headmaster had a fit and cancelled exit leave for the month. He also ordered the tuck shop closed for a week.

Of course, no one owned up. It could have meant expulsion. Some suspicions fell on the Fearsome Four because of our aversion to morning PT, but nothing could be proved.

No one was very anxious to find the bell—we were quite happy without it—but it was finally discovered hanging from a branch of one of the headmaster's apple trees.

'Must have been a ghost,' said Tata thoughtfully.

'It may have been Mr Sharma,' surmised Brian. Mr Sharma, our maths teacher, was known to walk in his sleep. And sleepwalkers did funny things sometimes.

'It could be Mool Chand himself,' suggested Cyrus Satralkar.

Mool Chand was the school chowkidar, who also had the job of banging the brass bell at appointed times.

'Why would he throw it away?'

'He must be as fed up with ringing it as we are with hearing it.' This was my theory. 'Perhaps he wants a rise in salary.'

The identity of the culprit remained a mystery. Happily, the senior hockey team went on a winning spree against all corners, and our month-end exits were restored.

But soon there was another sensation.

A girl was admitted to our class!

The boys were scandalized. No girl had ever studied in Bishop Cotton before. We protested.

'What's the problem?' asked Mr Knight, our class master. 'Haven't all of you seen a girl before?'

'But—but, sir . . .' Tata was our spokesman. 'How will we concentrate on our studies?'

'When did you *ever* concentrate on your studies, Tata?'

'Are we going coed, sir?' Adams wanted to know. He rather fancied the idea of having a girl, or girls, in our class.

'Not at all,' said Mr Knight. 'This is a special case. She is our bursar's daughter, and he can't afford Auckland House. So I'm sure you'll make her feel very welcome.'

The bursar, Mr Advani, was a popular man who also ran the school's tuck shop and allowed most of us a certain amount of credit. All our objections faded away.

At first, Sunita, our new entrant, was a bit of a distraction because, although she was very shy and demure, she had lovely curly hair (like Shirley Temple, the child film star), bright eyes, pink cheeks and a smile for everyone. All the boys were very polite and attentive to her, and Brian, in particular, was always ready to fill her inkwell or share his geometry instruments with her. His dark good looks and Dev Anand puff set him apart from the rest of the class, for most of us were a scruffy lot who did not attach much importance to appearance.

That was the age of inkwells and penholders with nibs that could be replaced. The fountain pen had only recently been invented, and it made quite a mess; biros, or ballpoint pens, were still in the future. What an antiquated lot we were! But then, Dickens wrote all his novels with a quill pen, and so did other great authors, and I was already something of a bookworm, reading Dickens and Stevenson and even Agatha Christie and P.G. Wodehouse.

There was no television in those days and, of course, no computers, but we could go to the cinema once a month. Everyone read comics— Batman and Superman and Green Lantern— but not many were reading books. We had to borrow one from the library every week, but these books usually went unread. I suppose it's much the same today.

Sunita was one of the few who read books, and sometimes she would discuss them with me. She'd enjoyed *Black Beauty* (the story of a horse) and *The Secret Garden*, both books by women, and we shared a weakness for Agatha Christie's detective novels. Sometimes we met in the library and would argue over the respective abilities of Hercule Poirot and Miss Marple. I think Brian Adams was a bit jealous of the attention I was getting from Sunita; he even started reading a little.

'And what are you reading, Brian?' I asked him one day.

'Never you mind,' he said, hiding the book from me. 'You're not the *only* intellectual in this school.'

I peeped into his desk later and saw that it was a book about Billy Bunter, the Fat Owl of the Remove (roughly our age), who ate his way through hampers of cakes, mince pies, buns, lemon tarts, candies and other delicacies, and survived to feast another day.

But there were no fat boys at Bishop Cotton. We were kept on a spartan diet. The school's policy was to keep us busy from morn till night, so that we did not have an opportunity to get up to mischief. PT, prayers, classes, meals. Classes again. Games (compulsory, of course). Homework. Supper. Bedtime. Lights out.

And then Fishy would be on the prowl, making sure that everyone was in bed and that no one was roaming about in the corridors and dormitories, pretending to sleepwalk. If someone was caught (usually Tata), he would pretend to sleepwalk. A school full of sleepwalkers!

This monotonous routine made some of us long to escape, to find some channel for our adventurous spirits. And this happened when the Fearsome Four discovered a tunnel.

4

THE TUNNEL

It was Cyrus Satralkar who discovered the disused underground drain. As a result of his discovery, we nicknamed him Christopher Columbus. He'd opened up a new world—in the form of an old drain.

Grass, weeds and rubble had blocked the opening of this disused channel, but when cleared away by the four of us, it revealed an underground tunnel that, at some time, must have gone somewhere.

Sundays were off days for the school staff and, therefore, for the rest of us, no PT, no games, no classes. We could read, indulge in pillow fights in the dormitories or wander about in the school grounds, but not outside them.

We had an entire afternoon to ourselves to explore that old drain, or escape tunnel, as we called it.

Cyrus, being the slimmest, was the first to advance some distance into its depths; when he got stuck, we pulled him out by his feet. We took turns going in and clearing away roots and loose stones. The drain was fairly well bricked up and in no danger of collapsing. It appeared to be inhabited by a family of rats. And if rats could survive in it, so could we. It was damp too, and our clothes were soon muddied and filthy.

It took us three Sundays to get to the end of the drain. We first emerged in a gully outside the school wall, a little distance from the

main gate. This wasn't a great distance—about the length of a cricket pitch—but it gave us a sense of achievement, a feeling of freedom. We were outside the school boundary!

Every Sunday, before the monsoon set in, we would visit our escape route and go down our tunnel, taking turns to lead the way. We had beaten the system—for a time, at least.

Then one day we were followed by Tata and Mirchi (Mirchandani), and where Tata went, trouble followed. He did not go looking for trouble. Trouble went looking for him.

Although the tunnel was the discovery of the Fearsome Four, we did not have any God-given right to it, and if others wanted the thrill of plunging through a dusty old drain, who were we to stop them? Mirchi, a skinny fellow, got through without any difficulty. Tata got through too but lost his spectacles in the process.

Coming out at the other end and seeing only a blurred figure standing in front of him, he gave a silly grin and said, 'See, I wormed my way through!'

'Yes, just like an earthworm,' said Mr Fisher, who was waiting there, cane in hand. He'd been keeping an eye on Tata that day.

All six of us were caned on the spot. Three strokes each on the seat of our pants. No exercise books for protection.

'Now off to your dormitories, and make sure you shower. Earthworms, the lot of you.'

We didn't stay to argue the merits of earthworms, those great tillers of the soil. But it didn't really matter. The monsoon broke a day or two later, and the drain was soon serving its original purpose—an outlet for runnels of rushing rainwater.

And the football season had begun.

5

BETWEEN THE GOALPOSTS

I was a goalkeeper again.

But being a football goalkeeper was very different from being a hockey goalkeeper. You were not encumbered by pads, and your hands were free. And the ball was different. It bounced, it flew through the air, it shot along the ground, it connected with your head. It was as large as your head—it had character.

And the goal was bigger too. It was a big leap from one goalpost to the other. It was another leap to tap the ball over the bar. There was a net behind you, and if you were a goalkeeper, you had to protect it, to keep away balls that came whizzing along the ground or floating through the air.

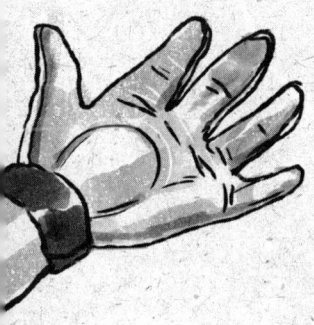

I loved standing between those two goalposts. It was my true home.

I was ready to dive around the stony ground of our grassless playing field. I did not mind scraping the skin off my knees and elbows. And I had a good left-footed kick and could send the ball beyond the halfway line.

Goalkeeping is all about anticipation—when to run out and punch the ball away, and when to stand firm and gather it neatly in your arms, holding it tight against your belly. You can't let it bounce away. An opposing forward will pounce on it immediately.

You couldn't keep me out of that goal. It was my domain, and I had no rivals.

And there was something special about playing in the rain.

Almost every afternoon the monsoon rain belted down, but that did not prevent us from trooping down to the field for a practice match or a house match or a game against another school. We were, of course, still juniors, but we took our games seriously and we liked to win.

Both Azhar and Brian were on the school team—Azhar a half back and Brian the right wing. It was good to have my friends playing beside me. Cyrus did not make the team, but he was always on the sidelines, cheering us on.

We did not have a real coach, although Dunda Hawkes was always around, giving us advice and doing his best to keep us fit. But football is a game of instinct, and if you love and cherish the ball itself, you will know how to deal with it.

As there was no television in those days, there were no big stars to emulate. We learnt about them from magazines and newspapers. There was a story paper called the *Champion* that came from England, which featured the exploits of a fictional goalkeeper called Flying O'Flynn. I wanted to fly like him!

Wet and muddy after a game, we would make for the shower room to wash ourselves down, and then to the tuck shop for sustenance in the form of hot pakoras or jalebis. One day Brian received a food parcel, and in it was a tin of Kraft cheese that had come all the way from Australia.

World War II had been over for more than a year, but some food items—butter, cheese, chocolates—were still hard to come by. Brian divided his Kraft cheese into four portions, and each of us had his share. Now, there was a friend!

*

We had a good team and we won our annual game against Sanawar, this time held on our own grounds. They brought some of their girls along as cheerleaders, but this time we were able to give a suitable response. Sunita appeared on the sidelines and screamed and shouted so vigorously that the Sanawar girls were stunned into silence. Bishop Cotton had a girl at last—a tiny one, but full of spirit!

We won some games, we lost a few. You can't have a game without losers; they are just as important as winners. Without them, you end up playing against yourself. And no matter how good you are, there will always be someone who is better than you.

We learnt that lesson when we went to play a game at Milsington, then a school for boys from poor families. But they weren't poor in talent. Their forwards made rings round us, and I had a busy time keeping the ball out of our net. I played the game of my life, even breaking a tooth when I dived at the feet of an advancing forward, receiving a boot instead of a ball in

my face. Oddly enough, that chipped tooth has remained in my mouth all these years. I think of it as my lucky tooth—even though we lost the match.

We managed to prevent them from scoring until the game was almost over. Then the ball came bouncing towards me—quite harmlessly, it seemed—and I stepped out to gather it, when it must have struck an uneven patch on that stony field, for it spun away out of my grasp and went into the net. We had lost the match, and for a day or two I was the villain in the eyes of everyone except my friends.

'Bond let in a goal!' This was the comment that was heard in the corridors and classrooms. 'We lost to Milsington—what a disgrace!' I felt like a criminal who had committed a terrible crime. And most of the school had not even seen the match.

I was mooning about in the library when Sunita came up to me and said, 'I saw the game the other day. They were too good for us, but you were terrific! You're a super goalkeeper!'

'Thanks,' I said. 'I did my best.'

And that's all that matters, isn't it? Doing your best.

All I'd wanted was a little praise for my heroic efforts. It had come from an unlikely person. But it compensated for all the criticism I'd received, and it made that broken tooth worthwhile.

And I knew I was still the best goalkeeper in Simla, if not the world!

6

15 AUGUST 1947

The football season was almost over. But it kept raining, which was fine when it meant cancelling morning PT. Not so fine when it meant curtailing those exits into town or trudging through a downpour in raincoats and soggy shoes.

The headmaster, in his wisdom, decided that the rainy season was the best time to hold our annual marathon. And many practice runs before it.

I hated the marathon. I saw no point in running around the mountain for a distance of some five miles, ending the race where it began—at the school gate.

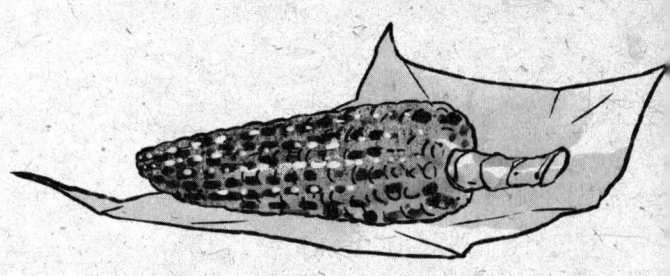

So at every race I loped along in a casual manner, stopping now and then to watch the monkeys gambolling in the trees or a rickshaw emerging from the mist (like the phantom rickshaw in Kipling's story), or taking a break to buy a roasted and salted bhutta. These little diversions meant that I would come in last, long after our junior marathon was declared over. Mr Fisher at the school gate would clap at my

arrival and say, 'Well done, Bond. You've come in first in the next race, ahead of the seniors.'

Azhar and Brian didn't mind winning races, but Cyrus would lag behind and join me in philosophical conversation as we ambled along.

'It's Independence Day next week,' he observed in the course of our last marathon run. 'Independence for India. How do you feel about it?'

'Okay,' I said. 'It had to come sooner or later. It's all about freedom. And everyone's afraid of Gandhi, although he's not much taller than you!'

'Will you be going away?' he asked, curious.

'Don't think so. Not unless I have to.'

'Azhar may be leaving. The country is being divided up, and his home is in Peshawar.'

'Why is it being divided?' I questioned.

'Don't know. You'll have to ask our leaders. It's a religious divide, it seems. But you and I shouldn't be affected. I'm a Parsi—and you, Ruski?' He always called me Ruski, although most of the boys used surnames when addressing each other.

'A bit of everything,' I said.

Cyrus knew more about the political situation than I did. Although I knew a bit about Gandhi and Nehru and other leaders, I had no real interest in politics. I would accept whatever came along. My stepfather was an Indian and a Hindu and he wouldn't be going anywhere, nor would my mother and small brothers and sister; in truth, there was nowhere for us to go.

Some of our teachers were going away, we heard. Mr Knight to England, Mr Brown to Australia. This was understandable. Rumours were rife that all schools teaching in English would have to close down. There was a lot of uncertainty in those days. No one knew quite what to expect . . .

*

On the fifteenth of August, that first Independence Day, we were roused by the ringing of the bell. No PT that morning. That was a good sign. We went into breakfast in a happy frame of mind, and as a special treat we were given laddoos, halwa and samosas, then marched up to town to take part in a flag-raising ceremony.

All this went off gloriously—or as gloriously as the rain would allow, for Nature waits upon no man—and we sang the national anthem as vigorously as any in the crowd. Unfamiliar with Hindi, we had been practising it for weeks! All the big speeches were being made in New Delhi, but we had our share of them too, and the massive crowd on the Ridge listened patiently, applauded generously and went home happily.

The entire school had attended the ceremony. We had worn our suits and ties and caps. The school cap, so British, so public school, was still a part of our uniform. On our way back to school we split into groups, and the Fearsome Four lagged behind. Brian took off to purchase a supply of roasted bhuttas. Munching happily, we marched on through the rain, singing a few songs of our own.

'Well, Adams,' asked Cyrus, 'how do you feel about being in a different country now? It's a new India, not British India.'

Brian shrugged. 'Can't say,' he said. 'We're leaving anyway.'

'And you, Ruski? How do you feel about it?' asked Cyrus.

'It will take time to sink in,' I said. 'Right now, the rain is the same as it was yesterday.'

7

THE LIGHTS GO OUT

And yet everything was changing—and the changes came fast and frighteningly.

With Independence came a division of the country. The familiar India of our maps and postage stamps and railway timetables disappeared overnight. Borders were drawn, two Pakistans were created—one in Bengal, the other in Punjab. Soon, entire populations were on the move. Homes were lost. And when homes are lost, there is conflict.

One incident led to another, one murder resulted in two. Killings had to be avenged, and vengeance led to revenge and more killings. Hindus and Sikhs fled to India, Muslims to what had been West Punjab or East Bengal. Across the north, trains came to a halt, passengers slain, railway platforms piled high with the dead. The violence spread like wildfire, even up to Simla.

There was a riot in the Lower Bazaar, and another in Chotta Simla, the area close to our school. One of the school bearers failed to turn up for work one morning; his multitasking body was found in a gully near the bazaar. Another fled to Kalka to see if his family was all right; he did not return.

Down in the plains there appeared to be no end to the violence, and parents were growing anxious. Fathers and mothers in distant Peshawar

and Quetta wanted their children to come home—but how were they to travel?

A decision was soon made. It was decided that the entire Muslim contingent would be evacuated—roughly one-third of the school.

Four or five army trucks were provided by the government, and these were manned by soldiers, both Indian and British. The convoy was to leave at midnight, when the town was supposedly asleep. It was all very hush-hush.

I was asleep when someone shook me by the shoulders, and I woke up to find Azhar leaning over me.

'We're off!' he said. 'We're going home. Under army escort. As far as the border, anyway. We'll be met on the other side.'

I leapt out of bed and got dressed, putting on my dressing gown instead of my coat. Everyone in the dormitory was up. Some were leaving, the rest of us wanted to say goodbye. Half-dressed, some in pyjamas, some in shorts, we straggled down to the first flat, where the trucks were waiting, being loaded with trunks and bedding rolls.

It was almost midnight. The rain had stopped, there was a rift in the clouds and bright moonlight shone upon the field.

Cyrus, Brian and I helped to load up the trucks. Dunda Hawkes was already in one of the trucks, making arrangements.

'We'll do it for you, sir.'

'No, I'm going with them. And I won't be back until I see the boys safely over the border.'

Dunda Hawkes had been deeply affected by the division of India. He was a simple man who,

like my father, had been to army school and spent most of his life in barracks or on the march. He had become a boxing champion and was responsible for making sportsmen and athletes out of most of us. He blamed everyone—the British, the Indian and the Pakistani leaders, the civil servants—for bringing about this upheaval in his school and in the land to which he had grown so attached.

Mr Fisher was among the boys, saying goodbye, giving advice and motivations.

'Mr Hawkes is going too, sir!'

'Can't stop him,' said Fishy.

Azhar was beside me, his arm around my shoulders.

'Time to say goodbye,' he said. 'I'll write to you. We'll meet again—some day, somewhere.'

Surely we would meet again. The world hadn't come to an end. But the light was going out in a lot of lives, and it would be some time before it came on again.

The trucks moved off silently.

We waved to Azhar—Cyrus, Brian and I. The Fearsome Four were down to three.

We watched the headlights of the trucks as they moved down the mountain road. Then we returned to our half-empty dormitories.

Mr Fisher did his rounds.

'Lights out!' he called. 'Lights out everywhere.'

The lights went out, one by one.

8

HAMLET WITH BRIAN

For a few days the school was in a state of suspense. Had the convoy got through to Lahore? Were the boys safe as well? Telephone lines were down—the postal and telephonic system had been disrupted. Dunda Hawkes had yet to return.

When he did come back a week later, he looked aged and worn out. The *dunda*, or stout stick, that we had known was now bending, about to break. He was told to rest, and Mr Brown, the senior master, took our early morning PT. There was no escape from those early morning exercises. Bending, stretching, leaning over backwards . . .

'Down on your haunches, Bond!'

'Arms above your head, Tata!'

'Get moving, Adams, or I'll make you stand on your head!'

Life was slowly coming back to normal, that is, the country was trying to find her bearings. But there were all those empty spaces in the classrooms and dormitories, and no one could be sure if they would be filled again.

The rains were almost over. A rainbow appeared over Tara Devi, the neighbouring mountain. Wild dahlias flaunted their many-coloured blooms on the slopes above the school. Sunflowers brightened up the headmaster's garden; he seemed more cheerful too. The school wasn't going to shut down.

We examined our tunnel. It had caved in during the rains. It was off limits now, and anyway, we did not have the heart to start tunnelling into it again now that Azhar had gone. Sometimes we don't really value our friends till we have lost them. Azhar's departure left quite a gap in my life. He had been someone to whom I could talk freely, someone to whom I could confide and share my dreams. Now there was only Brian, who liked to do all the talking, and Cyrus, who hardly spoke at all.

Towards the end of the year I received a letter from Azhar. I replied and gave him my home address, but I did not hear from him again. Perhaps the letters were lost, for there were many new borders. History, it seems, is all about shifting borders.

*

In early October we were given a week's holiday. Some of the boys, including Cyrus, went on a camping trip to Tara Devi. I spent a lot of time in the school library, reading the plays of Shaw, Barrie and J.B. Priestley. Brian dragged me out of the library and insisted that I accompany him into town.

'We'll go to the pictures,' he said.

And so we did.

We had a choice between seeing Esther
Williams in *Bathing Beauty*, Dilip Kumar and
Kamini Kaushal in *Nadiya Ke Paar* and Laurence
Olivier in *Hamlet*.

LAURENCE OLIVIER'S
HAMLET

I insisted on seeing *Hamlet*, and it almost resulted in the ending of our friendship. It wasn't a film for restless schoolboys. The acting was brilliant, but there were long passages of dialogue and monologue, and an atmosphere of doom and gloom ran through this tragedy of Shakespeare's.

When we got to Hamlet's soliloquy—'To sleep, perchance to dream'—Brian had literally fallen asleep, his head resting on my shoulder.

Afterwards he wouldn't stop complaining about how I'd spoilt his day by taking him to see Shakespeare when we could have enjoyed watching Esther Williams in her swimsuit doing acrobatics underwater. I apologized profusely and kept feeding him pakoras all the way back to school.

Bathing Beauty was no longer showing on our next outing, but I made up for everything by allowing him to take me to see *The Phantom of the Opera*. It wasn't as frightening as we thought it would be; instead it was full of

classical music, and, once again, Brian fell asleep halfway through.

We spent the rest of the holidays in school, kicking a football around or sitting in the tuck shop, consuming jalebis fresh from the pan.

The final exams were approaching, and we had to put in a certain amount of study. Also, the nights were getting cold, and the days chilly— early morning PT was more than ever a trial.

It had been a momentous year—a year full of incident, of friendships won and lost, of memorable hockey and football matches, of tunnels and canings, of the coming of Independence, Partition and of the school in turmoil. And now, suddenly, there was a calm, an autumnal calm, as if the elements themselves were tired of all this human excitement and wanted to slow things down with soft breezes and fewer hours of daylight.

Something had to happen.

9

GOODBYE, MR HAWKES

It was the unexpected that happened.

A part of the first flat's retaining wall, weakened by the heavy monsoon rains, gave way and came down with a thunderous rush of stones and rubble. It happened at night and no one was hurt, but the path to the field and the lower school building was blocked and had to be cleared.

Dunda Hawkes called for volunteers. Everyone volunteered. It meant missing classes for at least two or three periods.

Dunda Hawkes chose some ten or fifteen of the senior boys and put them to work. But old Dunda was no shirker. He was as active as any of the boys. Wearing first a vest, which showed off his bulging muscles, he seized the largest rocks and flung them aside as though they were tennis balls.

A boulder, larger than the rest, was resisting the efforts of two of the boys. Dunda went to their aid. Forgetting his age, he went down on his haunches, got his arms under the boulder and gave a mighty heave.

The boulder moved. It rolled away. And Dunda Hawkes sank to the ground, blue in the face, gasping for breath. He had brought on a heart attack.

The boys ran to him, lifted him up and carried, or rather, dragged, him to a corner of the field. Someone ran for water, someone else ran for the headmaster and someone for the school nurse. But Dunda Hawkes did not get up again. He died right there on his beloved playing field.

The school turned out for his funeral. The hillside above the little cemetery was packed with schoolboys, staff and servants, for everyone had loved Mr Hawkes, in spite of early-morning PT.

No bell rang that day, the school was so plunged into a period of gloom. The division of the country, the departure of so many boys and now the sudden death of someone who had seemed so permanent—as permanent as the school itself, and all it stood for.

But was the school permanent? Many of us wondered . . .

*

Back to the usual routine, we moved inevitably towards the end of the school term. Exams were in the offing, but in those far-off days we did not fear exams with the same intensity with which boys and girls must face them today. Most of us were making plans for the long winter holidays. And some, of course, were leaving for good.

I was looking forward to the three-month winter break with the same eagerness as the others. There were several cinema halls in Dehra, and I would definitely be frequenting them. There was a stream in the forest where a friend of mine went fishing, and I planned to join him. A bicycle awaited my arrival! And there was a bookshop where I could buy Penguin paperbacks and Collins Crime Club selections for two or three rupees each.

But it's unlucky to make too many plans.

With about a week to go before the school closed, Mr Fisher called me to his office.

'Some bad news for you, Bond. Well, nothing too awful, so don't look so worried. Your stepfather had a car accident, and he's recovering in hospital. At the same time your mother is due to have a baby. That makes things difficult for her. So she's asked me to keep you here in school for another week or two, until things have settled down at home. We don't usually keep boys on during the holidays, but as the office will be open and a couple of staff members are staying on, we decided that you could stay with us for some time.

You can take your meals in the staffroom. How's that?'

'It's very kind of you, sir,' I said, although I couldn't hide my disappointment.

'There have been some complaints about the food,' said Fishy, changing the subject. 'Have you any suggestions?'

'It's all right, sir,' I said. 'But we could have more of it.'

'More rice? More bread?'

'No, sir. Two cutlets instead of one.'

'That's a large cutlet you get. You'd prefer two small cutlets instead of one large cutlet?'

'Two large cutlets, sir.'

'I'll think about it, Bond. Your dietary suggestions are always welcome. So be off, and make sure you pass maths or you'll be in the same class next year!'

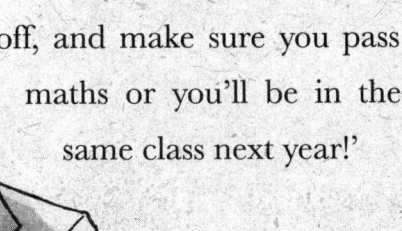

10

COMING ROUND THE MOUNTAIN

So I was condemned to an extra fortnight in school while everyone else left for home. Instead of being seen off with the others, I found myself on the station platform, saying goodbye to my friends.

'Poor Bond,' sighed Tata. 'Stuck in school for the holidays . . .'

'And having to eat with Fishy and the staff,' added Mirchi. 'Enough to kill one's appetite.'

Tata and Mirchi were both heading to Bombay for their holidays and would be coming back. In charge of the Bombay-bound party was Mr Advani, who was accompanied by his wife and daughter, Sunita.

'I hope you'll save many goals next year,' Sunita said kindly.

'Won't you be coming back?'

'Yes, but I'll be in the girls' school, as a boarder. I'll miss all of you—or most of you, anyway. I'll come around whenever there's a holiday.'

Cyrus and Brian were in another compartment, headed to Bombay too. Cyrus wasn't sure if he'd be returning, but he promised to let me know. Brian said he'd be writing to me from New Zealand. I knew he wasn't much of a letter writer.

'Send me lots of beautiful postcards,' I said. We shook hands. In those days we were not given to hugs and demonstrations of affection. But I loved my friends, and they knew it and loved me too.

The guard blew his whistle, and the small train moved slowly out of the station, the engine letting out steam.

Some of the boys were singing.

   We'll be coming round the mountain

   When we come, when we come.

   We'll be coming round the mountain . . .

The song died away, drowned out by the chugging of the engine.

   And I was still on the mountain.

*

Taking my meals in the staffroom was no problem. When a boy is hungry, he doesn't care who's watching. And the school was down to a skeleton staff.

   It was the dormitory that was a bit depressing. All those empty beds! No one to talk to. No pillow fights, no slippers flying through the air. I'd read a bit, then put the lights out

and lie there dreaming, the only company being
the caretaker's cat, who would prowl around all
night, hunting mice, until it, too, got sleepy and
made use of one of the beds.

During the day I would wander about on the playing field. The football goalposts were still standing, and I would place myself between them and make imaginary saves against an imaginary ball. Anyone seeing me leaping about, clutching or parrying an imaginary ball, must have thought I was mad.

And there was always the library. I had it all to myself. The sun came in through a large window, warming every corner of the room. Immersed in *The Pickwick Papers*, I joined Mr Pickwick and his friends on their journeys and adventures. They were good company.

Then, finally, after a week or two of my own company, a car and a driver arrived, sent from Dehra by my mother and stepfather. I was free to go home.

I went to Mr Fisher's office to thank him and to say goodbye.

'You'll be back next year, won't you, Bond?'

'Yes, sir, of course.'

'I'll do what I can about those cutlets.'

'Thank you, sir.'

'And we can both look forward to being a part of the new India. How do you feel about it?'

'It's fine with me, sir.'

'Good. And here's a book for you. I know you'll read it.'

He gave me a copy of M.K. Gandhi's *The Story of My Experiments with Truth*. I thanked him for it; I was to learn something about the saintly individual who had helped win freedom through non-violence and passive resistance. We could not foresee that in a month's time this great leader would lose his life to an assassin's bullet.

*

The car was waiting. I climbed into it, waved goodbye to the caretaker's cat and we drove away—round the mountain, down to the foothills, across the plains, through the forest, over two rivers and into the valley of the Doon.

I was going home and I was going to do all the things I wanted to do, and no one was going to stop me. I would play football in the maidan, go to the pictures, read detective stories, ride

around on my bicycle and eat a mountain of fresh, hot jalebis. I might even write a story about the Fearsome Four.

When you are only thirteen, you cannot do much to change the world around you. But if you keep dreaming and hoping and trying, you will eventually get what you desire, no matter how difficult a situation might seem and how uncertain the future.

ACKNOWLEDGEMENTS

Once again, a big thank you to Sohini Mitra, Janaki Sundaram and the Puffin team, and to Mihir Joglekar for his super illustrations.